Here to See It

Here to See It

Poems by

Benjamin J. Chase

© 2022 Benjamin J. Chase. All rights reserved.
This material may not be reproduced in any form, published,
reprinted, recorded, performed, broadcast,
rewritten or redistributed without
the explicit permission of Benjamin J. Chase.
All such actions are strictly prohibited by law.

Cover design by Shay Culligan
Cover art by Benjamin J. Chase

ISBN: 978-1-63980-122-0

Kelsay Books
502 South 1040 East, A-119
American Fork, Utah 84003
Kelsaybooks.com

For Mom and Dad

Acknowledgments

Grateful acknowledgment to these journals, which published the following poems, sometimes in slightly different form:

Pen Works: "Morning Wanderlust," "Edward Hopper's *Early Sunday Morning,*" "An Imagined Self and the Sea," "I Hear the Midwest"
Long River Review: "Commuter"
Freshwater: "Childhood Reflection"
Connecticut River Review: "Conference"
The Tulane Review: "Circumstantial," "The Work of Summer," "Edward Hopper's *Rooms by the Sea*"
Christianity and Literature: "A Rogue Goodness"
The Penmen Review: "Arrivals and Departures," "Departure"
Windhover: "Sins of Commission"
Fresh Ink: "Here to See It"
The Helix: "Don't Get Old"
The Aurorean: "A Goodbye, of Sorts"

A loving thanks to my wife, Cristina, for her continued support of my writing.

A special thanks to David Rigsbee for his editorial help and encouragement with this manuscript.

Thanks to the many professors, mentors, and peers at Wheaton College and Western Connecticut State University who helped me with my poetry.

Thanks to Silas Mullins and Chapter & Verse for providing a supportive writing community for me and so many others.

Thanks to all my family members, who have so often encouraged me in my writing life.

Contents

Morning Wanderlust	13
Edward Hopper's *Early Sunday Morning*	14
Commuter	15
Childhood Reflection	16
Love for Emily D.	17
Conference	18
Studying History	19
An Imagined Self and the Sea	20
Spring Comes to Monroe, Connecticut	21
A Pilgrim View	22
Circumstantial	23
A Rogue Goodness	24
The Work of Summer	25
One of a Kind	26
Edward Hopper's *Rooms by the Sea*	27
Arrivals and Departures	28
Jaws on Rewind	29
Humane Mouse Trap	30
Sins of Commission	31
Here to See It	32
I Hear the Midwest	33
Don't Get Old	34
A Backward Glance	35
Departure	36
A Goodbye, of Sorts	37

*Poetry is for me...a place to work out ideas, sure,
but more centrally the heart's matters...those
things the mind would deign to ponder,
or might be confounded by.*

—Dr. Brett Foster, 1973–2015

Morning Wanderlust

Like Ulysses strung to the mast
or his men with wax in their ears,
I cannot leave my rest
for sunlight or melodies of morning.

Sheets wound around me,
I'm held in the ship
of my bed, at the mercy
of its drifting.

I wander headlong
through destinies of sleep—
like a lotus-eater or one bewitched—
resisting the tides and shores of waking.

Edward Hopper's *Early Sunday Morning*

If not for a barber's pole
and a firm fire hydrant,
we might not know ourselves
apart, sleeping at the same angles

in the same blueprints
behind yellow shades
above window shops
on a Sunday morning.

If not for the grade of sky
and the angle of shadow
and the edge of another building,
we might be anyone.

Commuter

Today I watched a beetle
make the morning commute
in his sleek black suit,
hell-bent on the big city
of brush beyond the yard.

His antennas pointed forward,
and his limbs revolved
like little oars
on a warship.

I knew his locomotion
would lead somewhere,
but for now it seemed
like he'd never stop.

Childhood Reflection

I first found infinity
in the aisles of Kmart.

Mom was busy shopping.
I was multiplying
in parallel mirrors
by the fitting rooms.

Rapt, I watched
my every gesture
extend and diminish
across endless corridors.

I was transported,
but mom was unfazed
when she called my body
from its reflections with a word.

Love for Emily D.

Flight is a kind of falling
birds feather through the air—
like Love—a kind of falling—
catching us, unaware.

Conference

Teacher, parent, daughter.
We arrange our desks
in a scalene triangle.

Millennial, immigrant, teenager.
Our ternary talk breaks
binary at every turn.

Good cop. Bad cop. Criminal.
Roles may be subject to change
in time. Please come again.

Studying History

Before and after my class,
the students banter—
catechism style—
dealing despots
and dates, plagues
and reforms, trebuchets
and triumvirates.

It must be history
test day. It is.

Some squirm. Some puzzle.
Others burst with answers.
I join when I recall
a king or saint
of mention.

And so
the perennial history
of history
takes its rambling course.

An Imagined Self and the Sea

Sometimes I imagine
bearding myself
beyond recognition
and assuming some
short-voweled
northern accent.

I imagine loading
a little skiff
to the shriek of gulls
with a briny breeze
lashing my cheeks
and forehead.

I imagine living
a life by the lines
at my fingertips,
by what yields
or does not yield
by the day's end.

Spring Comes to Monroe, Connecticut

Today as I enter the salt-stained lot
with its dwindling drifts of snow,
the sky burns steady blue
and cirrus clouds wisp perfect white.
The lawns and woods are still gray brown,
but the sun is nearing its peak,
and the air is warming
behind cooler breezes.

As I pull around
to the ordering station—
iconic pink and orange—
I claim the new season by faith:
"Hello—I'll have a medium coffee,
iced, with cream and sugar."

A Pilgrim View

It's easier to remember
everything as grace
wholly beyond
my conceiving
on a swath of trail
on a side of mountain
I've never climbed
until now.

Dense mists rise
from towering firs
and tall balsamroots
sway about my path—
each an open blaze
of resurrection.

Circumstantial

Today, a boulder
refused to comment
on his glacial upbringing.

The moon was busy
bringing in the tides,
and her alibi held water.

The stars were too far
for questioning, and
the sun untouchable.

Everybody was in
on something big,
but nobody was talking.

A Rogue Goodness

There's still a rogue goodness
here. Weeds protruding

through cracking asphalt
in the parking lot of Super K,

for example. Thunderstorms,
abrupt and bellicose, interrupting

the little league championship
again, at the top of the seventh.

Or the forward-bent old man
inching his cart of recyclables

toward redemption,
speaking freely of Jesus

the way I can't.

The Work of Summer

—for Mark Chase

Mid-June, I lock up papers and red pens
to take up the carpenter's rules and measures.

I guide the whining saw along its line,
ply bursts of pneumatic nail guns,
and aim the grind of impact drivers.

I savor the careless order of the sites—
coarse subfloors, sawdusty surfaces, old figures
scrawled on studs and plywood panels.

But most of all, I love the balance of this trade—
each problem weighed in the mind, righted by the hands.

One of a Kind

I slump
in a hammock
between two ancient oaks.

It's afternoon.

A buck and doe
graze silently
in the meadow
beyond the stone wall.

Two whippoorwills
commence a conversation.

In the distance,
a lawnmower hums,
reckoning wild fields.

Alone, I nod,
accepting sleep,
aching a little
in the ribs.

Edward Hopper's *Rooms by the Sea*

As if we might wake
into perfect angles
in a living room
above the flood.

A door uncloses
sea and sky
to curling waves
and thunderheads.

Long shadows
climb the afternoon
in this curious place
we've always known.

Arrivals and Departures

Sometimes I spend an afternoon
on those half-padded seats
facing glass panels
in the arrivals section,
as if at the movie theater,
to watch the droves of people
entering my life.

It's cheating, I know,
a way to steal
an expectant glance
from a stranger
who might mistake me,
for an instant,
as a friend.

But I hold
no cardboard sign
and I incline
toward no one.
I just sip my coffee,
rattle my keys, and
after a time, I leave.

Jaws on Rewind

—inspired by Reddit user sixdoublefive321

Some stories are better backwards—
like *Jaws* on rewind
where that greatest white devours
the assembling scuba tank
before the bullet
enters Brody's rifle
and the skiff tips up
into sudden seaworthiness.

Keep watching
and our unlikely ally
returns each swimmer,
unscathed, to the public beach,
then vomits one last skinny dipper
just in time to find her lover.

Humane Mouse Trap

For a decade now, I've been leaving
packs of Pall Malls and lighters
on the floor of my front hallway.

My sticky note rules:
Do it on the back deck.
Don't let me see you doing it.
Clean up after yourselves.

So far, so good—
no messes, fires, or sightings.

Just diminutive coughing fits
from the pantry most nights,
and I can live with that.

Sins of Commission

Sometimes I tempt myself
when temptation isn't around.
What else is there to do?

It's like the girl I knew
who quit smoking.
I found her smoking.

"It's not that I needed *this* one," she said.
"I just couldn't stand the thought
of never smoking again."

Here to See It

I walk the end
of evening
on the edge
of a deep woods,
simply glad
the woods is here
and I am here
to see it.

On my way,
I watch and smile
as a water strider skims
the teeming surface
of his stream,
barely breaking it.

I Hear the Midwest

Sometimes now
when dark clouds collide,
crash, and strike,
like flint on flint,
I hear the Midwest.

I hear the tinny bells
of the train crossing,
and the first faint, then
surging metallic heave
of a freight train.

I find myself
on the football field
alone after dark
where my whole horizon
is a stretch of railcars.

The line screams
to a halt for a moment—
the crossing still clanging.

When it starts up again,
the first full tug
of locomotion
sends its strike,
boom, and jolt
across every hitch—

and suddenly, I'm back
in the stormy night
of right now.

Don't Get Old

"Don't get old, young fella,"
he quips across the waiting room
behind his book and reading glasses.

"I won't," I say, smiling
across the wide room,
which is only years.

A Backward Glance

One instant
as I was descending
another narrow pass
on the parkway
last night—

just one blur
of evening transit
among others—

I met
in my mirror
a tunneling canopy
of bare and arching
tree limbs
like a great kindling
stoking the setting blaze
of daylight.

Departure

Always, my father stands
in the gravel driveway
of whatever evening
I happen to be leaving.
Smiling, he waves.

He stands as if to say
everything else can wait—
he will be a father,
even into the cold night.
As if this were no departure.

A Goodbye, of Sorts

That bitter night
the air was so thin
our breath vanished
before our very eyes.

Sound itself
seemed to fall
straight to earth.
The air wouldn't carry it.

That's why I said
nothing to you,
but only turned
and walked away.

Then I heard the distant
scraping of a snowplow
clearing old avenues.
And then nothing.

About the Author

Benjamin J. Chase is a Connecticut native with an MFA in Poetry from Western Connecticut State University. His poems have appeared in more than a dozen literary journals over the years, including *Connecticut River Review, The Aurorean, Christianity and Literature,* and *Windhover.* He is a member of the literary reading group Chapter & Verse in New Haven, Connecticut, and he currently chairs the English department at Christian Heritage School in Trumbull, Connecticut. Besides reading and writing poetry, his hobbies include weightlifting, woodworking, photography, and motorcycling.

www.ingramcontent.com/pod-product-compliance
Lightning Source LLC
Chambersburg PA
CBHW071642090426
42738CB00013B/3187